T0078111

MARRIED BEFORE MARRIAGE

BECOMING THE WOMAN GOD CALLED
YOU TO BE IN LIFE AND LOVE

NICOLE RAE

WESTBOW
P R E S S®
A DIVISION OF THOMAS NELSON
& ZONDERVAN

WestBow Press books may be ordered through booksellers or by contacting:

WestBow Press
A Division of Thomas Nelson & Zondervan
1663 Liberty Drive
Bloomington, IN 47403
www.westbowpress.com
1 (866) 928-1240

THE HOLY BIBLE, NEW INTERNATIONAL VERSION®,
NIV® Copyright © 1973, 1978, 1984, 2011 by Biblica, Inc.®
Used by permission. All rights reserved worldwide.

ISBN: 978-1-9736-0862-2 (sc)
ISBN: 978-1-9736-0863-9 (e)

Library of Congress Control Number: 2017916609

Print information available on the last page.

WestBow Press rev. date: 10/21/2017

I dedicate this book to all women who
seek to be women after God's heart.

Thank you to my husband, who prays with me and
walks with me on my journey to be a woman after God's
heart. To my children, for whom I am an example,
thank you for your encouragement. To my mother and
my spiritual sister Vernita, who warred with me in the
spirit during my engagement, I love and appreciate you.

To all who poured into me and encouraged
me along my journey to marriage and
showing me God's way, I say thank you.

CONTENTS

INTRODUCTION

Marriage! I have dreamed about it since I was a girl. The thought of being loved by someone unconditionally for the rest of my life and living happily ever after put me in a dream world. As a girl, I watched all the movies with fairy-tale endings including *Cinderella*, *The Little Mermaid*, *Snow White*—all beautiful love stories about girls who spend the rest of their lives with their Prince Charmings.

Little girls all across the world are told to cherish love and anticipate the day they will be married. We were told to learn how to be domestic by cooking and cleaning. We were told to be prepared to have babies and settle down. We were told to depend on our husbands to be providers and take care of the bills while we take care of the house.

Then the world changed.

Women took to the workforce, and naturally, the landscape of the home began to change. Girls were encouraged to get educations so they could take care of themselves later. "Be independent!" they told us. Women began to tear down walls in the workplace and fight for equal pay and an opportunity to be successful in careers outside the home. The more equal we became, the less dependent on others we found ourselves to be. The dream changed from wanting a husband and a family to wanting a career and self-sufficiency. In all that change, however, a fact remains: many women, even successful ones, want their Prince Charmings and happily ever afters.

There is one problem, however. Somewhere along the line, the culture of female independence has muddied the waters and made it difficult for "independent" women to have successful, lasting relationships. I graduated from Drexel University and have a very successful career in project management; I've embraced female independence. I understand the woes of the independent mind-set and dating. It was not until I began to think differently that God allowed me to meet my Prince Charming, whom I call my Boaz, and am now married and living my happily ever after.

It was a long, hard road for me; I had to swallow some difficult pills along the way. I came to some realizations I didn't particularly care for, but I was a believer who wanted to follow God's plan for my life; I had to allow my mind to be transformed by his Word. Though it was difficult, it was worth it.

In this book, I share with you all I have learned in transitioning my mind-set to become an independent dependent; I realized I was married before marriage. Had it not been for the love of the risen king, Jesus Christ, and learning who he called me to be, his bride, I would still be in the cycle of meaningless relationships.

This book will be thought provoking and will challenge cultural norms, but I'm confident that as you read and pray, the Holy Spirit will enlighten you. When reading this book, be prayerful and ask God what he wants to show you about you and what he wants you to change. Use the questions at the end of each chapter to guide your transformation.

Though this is a short book, don't treat it as a quick read but as a guide to receiving what God has for you.

WISDOM

Blessed are those who find wisdom, those who gain understanding, for she is more profitable than silver and yields better returns than gold. She is more precious than rubies; nothing you desire can compare with her. Long life is in her right hand; in her left hand are riches and honor. Her ways are pleasant ways, and all her paths are peace. She is a tree of life to those who take hold of her; those who hold her fast will be blessed.

—Proverbs 3:13–18

The way of fools seems right to them, but the wise listen to advice.

—Proverbs 12:15

ADDICTED TO PAIN

Pain—an acute mental or emotional distress or suffering; trouble, care, or effort taken to accomplish something; usually localized physical suffering associated with bodily disorder characterized by physical discomfort.

B efore you start reading this book, let's discuss the concept of being addicted to pain. You might wonder why someone would be addicted to pain; nobody likes it, and nobody would intentionally put himself or herself in a painful situation. You're correct; nobody actually likes pain or chooses pain on purpose. However, pain affects a person's mind-set. If you're unaware of this, you may allow yourself to stay in a cycle of pain and not realize you have options. Sometimes, pain is all you know, so it's comfortable to live in pain even though it hurts. People in pain have habits that differ from those who aren't in pain, and sometimes when you step out of pain, you don't know how to behave. That can make it scary to change.

As you read this book, ask yourself how you can make this change. Think about everything you have been through and everything people have said and done to hurt you. Maybe you were molested, raped, or abandoned by your father. Maybe your mother was on drugs, or maybe you were on drugs. Maybe you were made fun of as a child. Maybe you think you're too fat or too skinny, too tall or too short. Maybe you were abused by a man you loved. Maybe your heart is broken. Maybe you don't realize you're broken. Many of us have no idea how broken we are.

My parents divorced and when it happened I was crushed. I was also molested, and for years, I kept that to myself because I felt ashamed—as if I had done something wrong. When I was a child, I was made fun of and often called fat, and even now, I struggle with the stigma of such name calling. I found myself eating more and more until I really became fat. Here I am now wondering how I got so big, but I'm working hard to lose the weight.

While I fasted before getting married, I reflected on my life and realized how much pain I had been carrying and that it had affected my decisions. In my pain, I created more pain by making bad decisions.

I learned that sometimes, we can be so accustomed to pain and strife that we make decisions that cause us more pain. Instead of choosing to be with someone who does not cause us pain, we run away or ruin the relationship because we're always waiting for the other shoe to drop. We're so hurt that all we expect is pain. And the pain is so real that we don't allow ourselves to believe there's light at the end of the tunnel.

No matter your situation, you can overcome it through the power of Jesus Christ. Realize you are in crisis; admit you've been hurt and have lived in a crisis mode for too long. Cry out to the Father in heaven for healing, forgiveness, and wholeness, and accept Jesus as your Lord and Savior. If you've already done this, consider whether you should rededicate your life to Christ. Just as love is a daily commitment, your relationship with Christ is a daily commitment; you grow and heal one day at a time.

If after reading this chapter you've decided you need to rededicate your life to Christ, or if you have never accepted Christ and you desire to have him transform your life, pray this simple prayer:

> Dear God,
>
> I acknowledge that Jesus is Lord. I believe he came to earth as a man and lived a sinless life. I believe he died in my place to wash away my sin, was buried, and rose on the third day.
>
> Father, I confess all my sins to you and ask you to forgive me for not obeying your Word. I am ready to trust you and to accept my role as the bride of Christ. I ask Jesus to come into my heart and live in me. In Jesus's name, amen!

The angels in heaven are rejoicing! Welcome to—or welcome back to—the family!

BEING INDEPENDENT

Independent—not dependent; not subject to control by others; not requiring or relying on others (as for care or livelihood); not looking to others for one's opinions or for guidance in conduct.

Female independence has become a huge part of American culture. The opportunities women now enjoy have made them less dependent on men for financial support. With the increase of government programs that support women, it becomes less and less of a requirement for women to have a male in the household. In truth, independence is great. Being able to take care of yourself and your household is a wonderful thing. Having an education or a career that brings you joy is exciting. But what is the cost of your independence?

A sad truth is that the rise of female independence in society has also resulted in the destruction of the family. This is not to say that men are not equally accountable for the destruction of the family, but I am not talking to men in this book—I'm talking to women. Female independence has contributed to women's diminished respect for men and to their inability to follow men as leaders. It has increased pride in women and accentuated masculinity in the female population. It used to be that there were male jobs and female jobs; now, women do much of the same work as men do—consider the "Anything you can do, I can do better" attitude.

This attitude, however, has thrown us off balance. There is nothing wrong with women being educated, successful, and self-sufficient. There is, however, something very wrong when our culture teaches us to believe we women are above or equal to men in terms of our *roles*. In the eyes of the Father, we are equal in person because God is no respecter of persons (Romans 2:11); however, there is a separation between the role women are called to versus the role men are called to. Today's society has blended the roles and stated that any gender can play any role; this gives way to sin and misrepresentation of God's plan for marriage.

Genesis 2:7, 20-23 reads,

> Then the Lord God formed man of the dust of the ground, and breathed into his nostrils the breath of life; and man became a living soul ... So the man gave names to all cattle, and to the fowl of the air and to every beast of the field; but for Adam there was not found a help meet for him. And the Lord God caused a deep sleep to fall upon Adam, and he slept: and he took one of his ribs, and closed up the flesh instead thereof; And the rib, which the Lord God had taken from man, made he a woman, and brought her unto the man. And Adam said this is now bone of my bones, and flesh of my flesh: she shall be called Woman, because she was taken out of Man.

If we are to understand who we were created to be, we need to understand the Word of God. Adam was created first; Eve was created to be Adam's helpmate. Keep the word *helpmate* in mind because we'll talk more about it later. But notice how we women were not created to be alone. We were not created to be independent; we were created to be helpmates and be dependent on God and man to be successful in life. Notice what I said there—dependent on God and man. In the independence movement, we learned not to rely on men or on God. In practicing independence, many women fail to give God his due glory or to call on his name in times of trouble. Somehow, we think we have accomplished everything on our own, without God or men, and we take pride in that.

We are in a season where God desires for us to transform our thinking about being independent, and thus, he put this book in my spirit. As a woman who says she's a woman of God—or a woman in general—I tell you that God is calling us to understand that while we can have a particular level of independence, we are still dependent on Him first and man second. God wants us to know that the spirit of independence can lead to sin. In 2 Timothy 3:1–5, we read,

> But mark this: There will be terrible times in the last days. People will be lovers of themselves, lovers of money, boastful, proud, abusive, disobedient to their parents, ungrateful, unholy, without love, unforgiving, slanderous, without self-control, brutal, not lovers of the good, treacherous, rash, conceited, lovers of pleasure rather than lovers of God—having a form of godliness but denying its power. Have nothing to do with such people.

Knowing that independence can lead to sin, you may have some questions about how we reach the place of independent dependence to avoid sin. Or you may wonder how you can respect and love a man the way God desires in a society that promotes female masculinity. You may ask what you need to do if you've been abandoned and forced into independence or what you need to do to draw closer to God's plan for your life and for love.

To answer those questions, we have to understand that we are dealing with an attitude of independence. There are two key drivers of this attitude: our upbringing and having been abandoned. To overcome this attitude and take on the attitude God desires us to have, we must recognize what drives this attitude of independence. Each woman's path to overcoming independence is different based on what drives her. A woman whose attitude is based on society or upbringing may involve the simpler act of intentionally changing her behavior. I say "simpler" with caution because changing behavior is not always simple. But a woman who was abandoned not only needs to change her behavior but also to overcome the hurt and pain of being abandoned.

A woman can be abandoned for many reasons. It may come from literally being left by parents or caretakers whether by choice, incarceration, or death. It can come from being rejected by friends and family. It can come from divorce. There are many ways she could end up feeling abandoned, and usually when women feel abandoned, they feel forced into self-reliance and the attitude of independence takes over them. Due to their abandonment, they feel they can no longer trust others.

This abandonment, though, heightens the desire for independence and can keep women on a course of repeated pain and rejection because they don't learn how to trust or continue to have their trust broken. Their judgment about whom to trust is usually off because of their feeling painfully abandoned.

No matter the reason for such feelings, the beautiful thing is that God has a plan for your transformation. First, if you haven't already, you need to accept Jesus as your Lord and Savior by believing in him and asking him to come into your life. From there, whether you have just accepted him or had accepted him long before this, you must repent. Repent for trying to live this life alone. Repent for being disobedient and not studying his Word. Repent for not trusting his plan for your life and trying to do your own thing.

You may have to repent for how you have treated others. If you've been abandoned, ask God to heal your hurt and give you comfort. Then decide to learn more about how God desires you to live and love and apply that to your life.

FOOD FOR THOUGHT

1. What is your personal view of independence? How does it shape your decisions and actions?
2. How have you treated men in your relationships? Despite what they did or said to you, what were your actions and responses?
3. Have you been hurt by society or have feelings of abandonment you haven't acknowledged? Do you harbor unforgiveness?
4. Have you been trusting God in your life and in your love life? Why or why not?

BEING DEPENDENT

Dependent—determined or conditioned by another; relying on another for support, etc.; subject to another's jurisdiction; subordinate.

As children, we were completely dependent on our parents or adult caretakers to supply all our needs—food, money, shelter, clothes, and emotional support. We have all experienced reliance on someone for something.

As children, we were also required to obey them and follow their instruction. We had to submit to them, their teaching, and their plans because as their children, we were subordinate to them.

When I was a kid, I couldn't wait to get older because TV portrayed adults as independent. I wanted to become independent because nobody could tell me what to do. But as an adult, I realize that though I have an element of independence, I still need to depend on someone. I've tried depending on boyfriends, friends, my parents, the church, the pastor, and you know what? In one way or another, they all let me down. I was searching for one person hoping he would have all I needed to live such a life. It's like the joke they make about dating—you date a handyman who can fix things, a rich one who can buy you things, a smart one who can teach you things, a handsome one to look good—different guys we wish we could roll up into one.

Just before meeting my husband, I hit rock bottom. Not a friend in sight. Parents miles away. Church folk who were there one day and gone the next. I had lost the man I thought I'd spend the rest of my life with. I was a smart, successful, independent woman who realized that in my independence, I had no one to depend on. But God! What the devil meant for evil, God worked for my good.

In that lowly place where I felt I didn't want to live another day, God reminded me I was not alone. He pursued me, loved me, and took control of my situation. He forgave my sins and for trying to live without him. I knew I needed him, but because I was living according to the world and not the Word, part of me believed I didn't need him and could make it on my own. I had no idea just how sovereign He was and is.

We think the world is in control because that's what we see, but when we begin to understand that the spiritual realm is real and that in fact it controls this earthly realm, we develop a different perspective on God and about being dependent.

Dependence is not about diminishing or compromising your value as a woman but rather posturing yourself in humility—not thinking more highly of yourself than you ought. It doesn't mean you cannot be confident, smart, or successful; it means that you understand there is always room for growth and understanding and that there is always something you can improve. It's about understanding the one who gives you your confidence (Proverbs 3:26), intelligence (Proverbs 2:6), and success (Deuteronomy 8:18 and Joshua 1:8).

If we claim to be in God, we must humble ourselves, seek his face, depend on him, and follow his commands. Jeremiah 29:11 reads, "For I know the plans I have for you, declares the Lord, plans for welfare and not for evil, to give you a future and a hope." In Proverbs 3:5–6, we are told, "Trust in the Lord with all your heart, and do not lean on your own understanding. In all your ways acknowledge him, and he will make straight your paths." We as believers are commanded to give our lives to the Lord. Having been created in his image, we are to live by the Holy Spirit and do spiritual things that will bring glory to the kingdom.

When I came to this understanding, I realized the marriage and the man I had been so desperately searching for had already come. "For your Maker is your husband—the Lord Almighty is his name— the Holy One of Israel is your Redeemer; he is called the God of all the earth" (Isaiah 54:5). In this scripture, we see that before meeting and marrying our earthly husband, we are married to Christ, and in that relationship, we learn to be wives.

Understanding I was first married to Christ opened my eyes to what marriage truly was. I was enlightened about women's dependence on men and how wives should treat their husbands. In learning to trust and be dependent on God, you will learn to be willingly dependent on man.

But the Bible tells us not to put our trust in man. If we put all our trust in man, it will be hard to be willingly dependent because in our human nature, we will always fall short. When we trust and depend on God as we depend on man, we are actually trusting God to guide man. So whether it be our bosses, our parents, or those we're dating, we trust God to guide them concerning us, and the more we do, the more willingly dependent on the person we become.

You may want to get a glass of water because here comes

a big pill I had to swallow. If you want to walk in God's way of love leading to marriage, you'll have to swallow it too. I present this message to you because God said in Romans 12:2, "Do not conform to the pattern of this world, but be transformed by the renewing of your mind. Then you will be able to test and approve what God's will is—his good, pleasing and perfect will." Here's what God told me: "I have created you to be a helpmeet" (We learned that in Genesis 2). "You must submit to your husband, you must pray for your husband, you must love your husband, and you must respect your husband."

We need to understand two things about submission. First, the Bible encourages submission from both the man and the woman to one another and to God. Second, we must understand that God created man to submit to him and woman to submit to man.

You might be wondering, *Why should I submit to a man?* This may be a challenging concept, but submission or obedience to your husband is what God requires. This goes back to the design of marriage, and it's an example of Jesus and his bride, the church. Just as the church submits to Christ, wives are to submit to their husbands. As the wives submit to God's will, they are practicing how to submit to their husbands. This submissive character is not something you wait to take on when you're engaged or married; even when you are single, you must exhibit these qualities even though society teaches you to turn this on only after you marry.

Learning to submit is difficult especially without practice. Submitting to someone else's vision when you have one yourself. Praying for someone when you don't feel like it. Loving someone who seems unlovable. Helping someone who doesn't appreciate it. Respecting those you feel aren't doing what you want them to do.

Let's be honest—there's no perfect man out there. Even

the one God designed for you isn't perfect; he'll fall short in some area or another that may make you want to reject God's role for you. And don't forget—you've been raised to be independent, so one wrong move, and your patience with the man you claim to love or maybe even the man God made for you but you haven't fallen in love with yet, and it's over.

This is when we must remember that even before we marry, we're married to Christ. Submitting to our husbands is not about them but about our relationship with God. In our premarital independence, we need to build our relationship with God and understand that we're dependent on him. When we marry, we are still dependent on God but become dependent on our husbands; as such, there's no room for the worldview of independence.

How many of us have missed God or missed the man God had in mind for us because of our unbiblical view of independence? My independent mind-set and my experiences, pain, and lessons learned almost made me miss my husband, but praise God—he woke me up before it was too late.

Don't allow yourself to miss God and what he has for you because your definition of independence is based on a worldview or any view not based on the Word of God. As a woman of God, you are called to be in the world but not of it (John 17:16).

FOOD FOR THOUGHT

1. Have you missed opportunities to live with and for God because you were too busy being independent?
2. Are you dependent on God to provide your every need? Including providing your husband?
3. Do you trust God's timing, or are you trying to move on your own time?

4. Think about your past relationships. Was there a reoccurring issue that suggests God was trying to change you before setting your husband before you?

5. Are you willing to acknowledge your shortcomings and prepare to be a wife?

BEING A BRIDE

Bride—a woman just married or about to be married

The parable of the ten virgins tells us much.

At that time the kingdom of heaven will be like ten virgins who took their lamps and went out to meet the bridegroom. Five of them were foolish and five were wise. The foolish ones took their lamps but did not take any oil with them. The wise ones, however, took oil in jars along with their lamps. The bridegroom was a long time in coming, and they all became drowsy and fell asleep. At midnight the cry rang out: "Here's the bridegroom! Come out to meet him! Then all the virgins woke up and trimmed their lamps. The foolish ones said to the wise, "Give us some of your oil; our lamps are going out." "No," they replied, "there may not be enough for both us and you. Instead, go to those who sell oil and buy some for yourselves." But while they were on their way to buy the oil, the bridegroom arrived. The virgins who were ready went in with him to the wedding banquet. And the door was shut. Later the others also came. "Lord, Lord," they said, "open the door for us!" But he replied, "Truly I tell you, I don't know you." Therefore keep watch, because you do not know the day or the hour. (Matthew 25:1–13)

Imagine how these women, these brides, must have felt being unprepared for the bridegroom. Ask yourself, *Am I ready for my bridegroom?* In your unmarried state, are you ready for your bridegroom, Jesus Christ? Are you ready for the earthly bridegroom God has in store for you?

Being a bride involves so much more than just planning the event, selecting a dress and a place for the wedding, and getting your hair done. Being a bride is a call to prepare for your marriage. As women of God, whether engaged in the earthly realm or not, we are brides of Christ waiting for his return and should prepare for that. The five wise virgins made sure they were prepared so they wouldn't miss their groom. They were also steadfast in their preparedness; they didn't share the oil they themselves needed.

You might want a groom, but how are you preparing for one? In the same way you prepare for Christ, your bridegroom, you should be preparing for your earthly groom. This means being thoughtful about your dating activities and not giving yourself away to the wrong ones and ending up broken. It's a matter of keeping yourself pure in thought, spirit, and body and not defiling your marriage bed. It's loving yourself and learning to love others as yourself. It's treating people with respect and carrying yourself with respect. It's about covering your future husband in prayer even now. If you're not willing to do this, why do you consider yourself ready to be a bride?

In previous chapters, we talked about being independent but understanding we're still dependent. An independent woman who doesn't realize her dependence on God or her future husband will say, "I can date whom I want, sleep with whom I want, treat people however I want, be disrespectful, and pray only when I feel like it." This thought pattern can be caused by defenses we have set up because of mistrust, pain, or hurt, but in the end, we make ourselves believe that because we're independent, nobody controls us but us.

A woman who recognizes her dependence on God and her future husband but maintains a level of independence while recognizing boundaries will ask, "How can I serve God and my future husband?" She will ask, "How can I use my personal achievements to bring glory to the kingdom and support my future husband? How can I uplift him with my words and my experiences?" A woman in tune with her dependence will grow her relationship with God and grow in her attitude toward her future husband so he will feel the conviction and freedom to lead her.

Prior to my wedding, I fasted for forty days; I turned down certain foods, turned off the TV, and turned away from social media. It was one of the most difficult times of my life, but it was necessary because marriage is a new dimension in life; it's in the spirit realm and is nothing to be toyed with.

I fasted because I wanted to draw closer to God; I wanted him to instill in me all I needed to be the best godly wife I could be. During my fast, God put me in a position where I had to continuously be in his presence praying not just for myself but also for my now husband. Just before we were married, I was desperate and needed God to be with me or I would have lost my mind and possibly my husband. Just before we married, we asked hard questions to ensure we were making the right decision and doing it God's way.

As brides (and grooms), we are called to invest in our wedding days and then in our marriages. Today, so many spend tons of time and money planning for the celebration but barely any time planning to be married. And then they wonder why they end up divorced. People notice the details of your wedding day including the colors and flowers; they also notice the preparation you put into your marriage. People may not admit it, but they go to weddings, watch the couples, and guess how long their marriages will last.

Couples who didn't put much time into marriage preparation or who didn't commit fully to the process are more easily spotted; others can at times sense discord even at the wedding. Couples who put in the effort and thoughtfully prepared for marriage are notable for their great show of unity and love.

In preparation for our wedding, my husband and I sought counseling, read books, and made a point to pray with one another. We even continued counseling in the weeks following our marriage, and I believe that was an essential element in our marital success. Our wedding day was beautiful not just because we had planned for the day but also because we had planned for growing together afterward.

Planning for your marriage starts with changing your mind-set and opening yourself to the transformational power of God. In this book, we are touching on areas in our lives that keep us from having the mind of Christ, things like hurt, pain, loneliness, and more. These things can keep us from trusting in God, which keeps us from trusting in man.

When we allow God into these areas of our lives, he will heal us; as he does, and as we get to know him better, our mind-sets will grow and change.

Whether you are single, in a relationship, or engaged, you can prepare yourself for your groom by understanding that though you may not be married in the earthly realm, you are nonetheless married in the spiritual realm to Jesus Christ. You want to be prepared when Jesus comes, so you do prepare for that and trust it will happen.

You'll be tested and tried as you prepare. You'll be tempted to do what you have always done, and you may even get discouraged and think God just hasn't designed you for marriage. Perhaps he hasn't, but either way, you must trust God. Give all your concerns about being a bride to the Lord. After you are a bride, you'll be a wife and have a critical role to fulfill. If it weren't a critical role, there would have never been an Eve—only Adam.

FOOD FOR THOUGHT

1. Do you want to be married? If so, how have you been preparing for marriage?
2. Do you understand your role as the bride of Christ and see how that corresponds to being a bride in the earthly realm?
3. Are you willing to commit yourself to proper dating, purity, love, respect, and prayer?
4. Do you trust God in the midst of it all?

TRUSTING GOD

Trust—assured reliance on the character, ability, strength, or truth of someone or something; one in which confidence is placed.

Dependence on God will sustain you until God finishes preparing your future husband and you for marriage in the earthly realm. Today's world tells us we're in control of our destinies, that we can do whatever we want whenever we want. It says whenever we feel we're ready, we can settle down and have a family. The world makes us believe everything happens in our time, so when it doesn't, we get upset. We try to do things differently to achieve our goals. When it comes to dating, that may mean settling for anyone just to say we have someone.

At times, we settle because we lack self-esteem or because we don't know our value, or have been abused, or we've lost ourselves and don't know who or whose we are. We have to press through such moments and draw closer to God so he can remind us of his abundant love for us and how valuable we are.

The person I just described was me. I told myself I was going to be married by age twenty-two and have my first child by age twenty-five. I did everything I could to try to make that happen, but I settled. I ended up with a child out of marriage and a relationship with someone with whom I was incompatible. I'm still experiencing the challenges of trying to be in control, but I'm learning.

The truth is that God is in control of everything! Even when you think you're in control or someone else is in control, it's because He allowed you or them to believe that. Let me be clear—God does not allow you to hurt or feel pain because He doesn't care. Sometimes, it's a choice you've made, and we all make some bad choices. Either way, everything God allows serves a purpose for building you up into who he has called you to be.

Sometimes, your testimony isn't for you; it's to help someone else see that you were able to overcome your difficulties and be encouraged by that. Many times in the Bible, God allowed things, and they always worked for the good of his kingdom. Look at Job and all the turmoil he went through because God allowed it to happen. How about the Israelites and their many desires and ways that were contrary to the doctrine of God? He allowed it all; it wasn't without consequence, but he allowed it. Since Adam and Eve, we've had free will because of their sin in the garden. All these stories of free will whether they made the right or wrong choice ended up playing a critical part in God's plan.

The garden shows us that trusting God has been an issue for us since the beginning, but we have also seen that believing God is in control is a critical part to trusting him. Many of us don't trust God because we don't believe he's truly in control. When we believe God is in control, something happens in us; we give him our problems and issues. Sadly, it takes times of desperation for many of us to give them to God and trust him to handle them.

What God wants you to learn from this book is that no matter the issue—big or small—God has a hand in it and should be trusted. Many have heard the saying "Everything happens for a reason," but what's the basis for that statement? Do they believe random powers cause things to happen, thus making that statement true, or do they believe God's sovereignty is the driver behind everything happening for a reason?

God's sovereignty is stated multiple times in the scripture, including 1 Chronicles 29:11–12.

> Yours, Lord, is the greatness and the power and the glory and the majesty and the splendor, for everything in heaven and earth is yours. Yours, Lord, is the kingdom; you are exalted as head over all. Wealth and honor come from you; you are the ruler of all things. In your hands are strength and power to exalt and give strength to all.

It took me a while to realize that God is sovereign and in control. Even before my husband and I were engaged, God began calling on me to trust in him. As was the case with my previous relationship, I found myself putting my faith, trust, and hope in the man I was with. Somehow, I thought he would supply all my needs, but when he couldn't live up to the task, I thought, *This can't be what God had in mind for me.* I had already prayed and talked to God about my desire to be married and have a relationship pleasing to him, and he had already confirmed in my spirit that my now husband would be just that. But when I began to put my trust in my husband, I almost didn't marry him because he fell short of my expectations.

When I cried out to God about what I thought would end up another failed relationship, he asked me, "Why are you putting your trust in him and not me?" I had to quickly check myself. We can expect certain things from men such as respect, love, kindness, and honesty, to name a few good qualities, but we cannot expect men to be solely responsible for making us feel confident, joyful, or treasured, again, to name just a few. These things come from knowing whose you are, putting your trust in God, and allowing his Word to define who you are and give you strength: "Trust in the Lord with all your heart and lean not on your own understanding; in all your ways submit to him, and he will make your paths straight" (Proverbs 3:5–6). The scripture doesn't say trust in him sometimes or when you feel like it. It doesn't say, "Trust me when you can't trust your man or anyone else." The word says to trust with all your heart and in all your ways.

We must trust God to send us the right man at the right time and trust him to carry the relationship through to marriage. Then after marriage, we must trust him to keep us married.

Unfortunately, my parents divorced, so I already had a tainted view of marriage; at one time, I gave up on the whole idea of marriage. Eventually, my mind changed because I became captivated with the concept of marriage. I didn't want to be alone, and I wanted children, so it felt right to be married. Honestly, I wanted to be married just to be married. I cared more about the wedding, the ring, the dress, and the kids than I did about the marriage.

To achieve what I wanted, I started walking out my own plan to get married the way I thought it should go. I didn't worry about divorce. I thought, *Who cares? You get married.*

You try it, and if it doesn't work out, you get a divorce. However, as I drew closer to God and began to trust him, he changed my mind about marriage, and my plan was suddenly no longer acceptable. The closer I got to him, the more I wanted to be part of his plan, not my own, for my life. I came to understand that what he had for me would be far better than what I could do for myself. I decided to follow his plan.

I can't say this will happen to everyone, but the moment I said yes to God's plan, I met my husband. He was and is everything I could have asked for and then some. And marriage was on his mind. We dated to determine if we were suitable for each other. This man was serious; he had his list just as I had mine. Despite my best effort to be just friends, he pursued me and changed my mind.

Soon into our relationship, we realized that this was it—he would be my husband and I would be his wife. I was excited, but then it hit me—I had no idea how to be married. However, I heard God say, "Trust me." He reminded me that I was already married to Jesus Christ and that the lessons I had learned in my relationship with Christ I could apply to my marriage. He revealed to me the meaning behind being a wife and being a helpmeet suitable for my husband. He gave me revelation on being a Proverbs 31 woman.

God showed me once again that it was not about me and my thoughts or me trying to be a wife on my own but about trusting him to mold me into the wife I needed to be. Just as God makes husbands suitable for their wives, he makes wives suitable for husbands, but we cannot embrace our roles as suitable helpmeets if we don't trust God.

Through the process leading from courting to engagement and from wedding day to marriage, we have to trust God! Even after God got my husband to propose, we still faced challenges. That's because the devil hates marriage. Up to now, he's been successful at destroying it before it starts by telling women they were independent and don't need God or man. He's destroyed it by causing you to be so independent that you can't keep a man.

When my husband and I got to the point of engagement, the enemy stepped his game up. People from the past started popping up; the enemy knew right where to hit me. He began playing on all my past hurts. But God! I remained grounded in God. I turned over every attack to my Father, and he handled it.

At one point when we were engaged, it seemed my husband didn't want to marry me. He wasn't fulfilling the duties I felt he had to in order to prove marriage was what he wanted. We had picked a venue, set a date, and created a guest list, but then, he left many tasks for the last four months. There we were in crunch time, and he was still trying to find someone to counsel us because the pastor who was supposed to marry us fell through. I was still trying to get addresses for invitations and still trying to get his people to get fitted for tuxes and purchase dresses.

All these challenges caused me to question his intentions and his desire to marry me. He was so involved in running his business six days and sometimes seven days a week that we had hardly any time for counseling, date nights, and family time. I know that in his mind, all of that was required, and in a sense it was. He didn't want to marry me but not be able to provide for me or for our family. I'm grateful for that, but I'd be lying if I said his preoccupation with that didn't strain our relationship or cause me stress.

Just as I am learning to be a wife, God is teaching him to be a husband. In all this, all I could do was trust God, but trust was hard for me. But I trusted God one day at a time, one challenge at a time, and as he brought me through, I realized I was learning to trust. Eventually, it became easier to trust him. Learning to trust God through that experience showed me that it doesn't always go the way we want it to go, but that doesn't mean he's not moving. He showed me that my husband wasn't perfect but then neither was I. He showed the importance of having godly premarital counsel and having godly married couples around us to mentor and pour into us.

Our premarital experience was a tremendous faith walk in every way from growing together as a couple to paying for the wedding and not going into debt to do so. It was nothing but God and his favor that caused that to happen.

Now that we're married, my faith walk continues, and I praise God I had the opportunity to practice being married before marriage.

FOOD FOR THOUGHT

1. Have you been trusting God? Have you been doing so wholeheartedly or just partially?
2. What do you need to give over to God? What have you been holding onto and need to let go of?
3. What plans have you made that you need to cancel to walk in his will? Have you been ignoring all the signs God has given you?
4. Do you feel you need to settle? Do you know whose you are and how much you are loved?
5. Are you willing to give him your "dating" life and trust him?

APPLICATION

Whatever you have learned or received or heard from me, or seen in me—put it into practice. And the God of peace will be with you.

—Philippians 4:9

COURTING

Courting—to seek to gain or achieve; al-
lure, tempt; to act so as to invite or provoke;
to seek the affections of; especially to seek
to win a pledge of marriage.

We just spent time gaining some wisdom and insight
from the Lord; we know we are dependent on him
and have to decide to trust him. If we trust him, that means
we have to trust him with our love lives; we have to turn
them over to him.

In this chapter and those that follow, we'll discuss apply-
ing the principles of God to our lives starting with courting.
The goal of dating or courtship is to find a spouse. The
difference is that dating speaks to the worldly way of finding
a spouse whereas courtship speaks to the method of finding
your spouse while maintaining blamelessness in the sight
of God.

Courting goes against social norms and even calls for us
not to engage in dating until we feel ready to consider marriage. Romans 12:2 tells us, "Do not conform to the pattern
of this world, but be transformed by the renewing of your

mind. Then you will be able to test and approve what God's will is—his good, pleasing and perfect will."

Before you can consider courting, you need to understand what it is. I attribute my success in identifying my husband to my choosing to court instead of to date. Courting causes you to determine what exactly you desire. You decide if you want to be married or not and then step out with a set of standards based on that.

I'm not saying go out on your first date and dive into these deep, heavy questions about the man's ideas about marriage, but I am saying you should have that conversation sooner rather than later—definitely by your third date.

When people decide to court, they do so to determine whether they're suitable marriage candidates for each other. Before they can do that, they have to know what they want. It requires a period of growing friendship, fellowship, and romance. Dating says the moment you meet, the relationship becomes sexual, which means one or both of you are just wondering if the relationship will result in sex; there may or may not be any real desire to get to know the person. Too often, we fall into the traps that dating sets, which is sex before getting to know the person, but we'll discuss more about sex and purity in a later chapter.

If your desire is to be married, courting provides you an opportunity to make a wise, informed decision about marriage without the agony of a messy breakup or soul ties, that is, spiritual connections to others that can be good or bad. Courting is in fact when you form a deeper relationship than just friendship, but it's not the same as what the world calls dating. Generally, when courting, you're more cautious with your heart because you understanding your goal.

So why court? Why can't you just date and have the same goal? Courting is different from dating in that dating tends to be more intimate right out of the gate. As soon as you exchange numbers, you set a time to meet—just the two of you—at a restaurant, a movie, at one or the other's home, or wherever. Dating from the beginning requires exclusivity; on the other hand, courting doesn't move so quickly into the one-on-one meetings but rather finds joy in gathering with others or being out in places that are less intimate. This process gives you an opportunity to get to know the person without the pressure of being one on one; you observe him interacting with others. How many of us have fallen for guys because they treated us so nicely, but then they turn out to be mean to others and we wonder how long it will be before they treat us the same way?

Whether you date or court, you want to protect your heart. Too often, we give pieces of ourselves away and wonder what will be left for our husbands. Each time we give our hearts or bodies away, we give away a piece of the gift God created for our husbands. I had been guilty of this too, and it's in large part why I decided to act differently. We go on and on about how much we deserve from our husbands or husbands-to-be, but what are we doing to ensure they receive the same? Does your husband not deserve your best as well?

Courting gives you an opportunity to guard your heart while allowing yourself to grow with the other person. It also provides a clear conscience about your premarital behavior and glorifies God in your relationship. When you're courting someone, your goal should be to point him toward God so he will grow in God.

Courting doesn't seek to stifle feelings of affection; rather, it challenges you to submit your feelings of affection and love to God so he will grow and guard them. The purpose of courting is also to ensure that you are not misleading the other person about your intentions; your intentions and relationship goals should be clearly defined. This is another difference with dating; when you're just dating, you don't define your intentions, and that can lead to heartbreak and wasted time.

If you've decided that courting is a better option for you, you may be wondering how courting starts and progresses. It begins with prayer! You should pray about your readiness for courtship and ultimately marriage to determine what your intentions are at the beginning of a new relationship. Your prayers should also include the person you're thinking of courting or are being courted by. If you haven't defined your current situation as courting, that's okay. Take time to pray about the person you are with. It's less about what you call it— courting or dating—and more about what you do to develop that relationship. No matter what you call it, prayer is a critical piece of it to ensure you get exactly what God has for you.

You should pray that your courtship will be pleasing to God. The Bible says in Ephesians 6:18, "And pray in the Spirit on all occasions with all kinds of prayers and requests. With this in mind, be alert and always keep on praying for all the Lord's people." Our love life is something we should pray about rather than trying to bring it to life on our own.

When it comes to courting, the male should be the initiator. Proverbs 18:22 tells us, "He who finds a wife finds what is good and receives favor from the LORD." You're worth finding; it's not your responsibility to go looking for a man or find a husband. It's the male's responsibility to lead on biblical fellowship, initiate meaningful conversation, and initiate romance in the courtship. This doesn't mean that as women, we can never initiate activities, but the man should be the primary initiator in courtship.

Though at times this is difficult, it's our responsibility to match the pace the male sets. Too often, we women can outpace men in relationships; we begin taking relationships more seriously than they do and begin to drive the relationships.

Sometimes, this works in our favor, but I would say more often than not it doesn't. In the end, we realize we were more into a relationship than a man was and then our hearts break.

This behavior can also make a man feel that his value is diminished and that he isn't respected as the head. A man who doesn't feel he's leading the relationship with his woman will either never marry her or marry her and have that marriage fail. Never give into the temptation to take the lead in driving and defining the relationship. If you do, you'll blur the lines between your God-given role in your relationships and will wonder if what you're doing is glorifying God.

Patience is a virtue! Our responsibility is to focus on being married before marriage. Remember—husbands find wives. We do not become wives when we start courting or when we get married. Up until the time we actually say I do to our husbands, we are brides of Christ. This doesn't change after marriage, but after marriage, we have earthly husbands, and our roles as wives should resemble our roles as brides of Christ.

If you're a male reading this book, don't mistake a lack of pep in your step for patience. If God has prepared your heart for marriage and for a particular woman, don't let your opportunity pass you by. True love is patient, but it doesn't torture you with waiting.

Here are some tips to be successful in courtship.

- Recognize that the joy of intimacy is commitment.
- Treat each other with holiness and sincerity.
- Seek counsel from parents, friends, and church leaders.
- Have appropriate pace, focus, and space.
- Don't try to rush or force yourself into each other's lives.

- Focus on getting to know each other before you talk about the relationship and its progression.
- Gradually make space for each other; don't try to monopolize each other's time.
- Be faithful to current relationships and responsibilities.
- Never use spiritual activities to gain more intimacy than appropriate.
- Set boundaries to prevent sexual sin; perhaps no kissing, cuddling, or late-night visits.
- Our primary source of accountability should be to members of the same sex.
- Don't offload all your hurts/shortcomings from previous relationships on the person you are courting; be thoughtful about the information and details you share.
- Try not to take the place of God in that person's life.
- Be a good listener; that's the true sign of authentic courtship.
- When you ask a question, absorb the answer and respond thoughtfully. Note what was said and how. Ask follow-up questions for clarity, and care more about the other's opinion than your own.
- Remember that men were created first to be leaders and initiators. Women were created to help men fulfill the mission God has given them. Women are meant to complement, nourish, and help men.

Until you're married, you're single, and you are a member of the body of Christ. If you aren't in a courting relationship, do your best to look at others simply as other brothers and sisters in Christ. Don't be blind to opportunities to court, but recognize that to glorify God in the premarital status, you have to be intentional in thought and behavior.

If you meet a man who isn't saved, pray for him! Don't assume that a man you met in church is saved. No matter where you met someone, if he is not saved, you cannot change him or force him to become saved. This is where you have to trust God to do a work in him and draw him into the kingdom. You could be the person God sent to him to plant or water the seed in him, but don't force it. If he shows no interest in being saved, pray and ask God if he is the man for you. The Bible tells us we should not be unequally yoked, and we know God has amazing plans for us, but I cannot tell you to be or not be with someone who is not saved. Only God knows the plan for your life and the life of the person you're seeing.

Use your single status to draw closer to God and glorify him with your life. Each stage of your life whether you're single or married comes with responsibilities, joys, and tribulations. Choosing to live a single life that keeps Jesus at the center will equip you to be the best wife you can be when the time comes.

FOOD FOR THOUGHT

1. Do you want to be married? If so, are you ready? Do you understand what it means to be married? Are you prepared to be whom God has called you to be as a wife?
2. If you are in a relationship or planning to be in one, have you ever discussed marriage? Are your intentions and his intentions clearly defined? Do you honestly feel the relationship moving in the direction the two of you have agreed it would go?
3. What's more difficult—staying where God is saying you shouldn't be, or walking away, letting God heal your heart, and waiting for the one God made just for you?

PURITY

Purity—the quality or state of being pure;
free from what vitiates, weakens, or pollutes;
containing nothing that does not properly belong; free from moral fault or guilt;
marked by chastity; ritually clean.

I 'll tell you that I didn't keep myself pure as I should have
before marriage. I did have premarital sex that resulted
in a child, and my husband and I had premarital sex before
making the decision to maintain our purity before God.

That said, I write this chapter not as one who has lived
a single life of complete purity but as someone who has had
to deal with and learn from the consequences of not living
a life of purity.

I wish I'd known better before I lost my virginity. I wish
someone had taught me what keeping my virginity really
meant. It's not merely abstaining from sex; it's keeping your
heart pure and free from soul ties. Purity is more than just a
matter of not having sex; it means keeping your spirit, mind,
and body pure so you can keep yourself healthy physically,
emotionally, and spiritually. Understanding that purity deals

with the totality of you as a person, I'll focus on purity from the standpoint of premarital sex.

The world has told us that sex before marriage is good, that it's okay to have multiple sexual partners and to explore our sexuality. Sex is truly a beautiful thing; it was created by God for our enjoyment but only after marriage. Many passages in the Bible talk about sexual immorality and fornication; I believe 1 Corinthians 7:2 sums it up very well: "But since sexual immorality is occurring, each man should have sexual relations with his own wife, and each woman with her own husband." This scripture indicates that God's design for sexual pleasure is indeed meant for marriage. If you don't believe me, read Hebrews 13:4: "Marriage should be honored by all, and the marriage bed kept pure, for God will judge the adulterer and all the sexually immoral." Every time we lie with someone who is not our husband, we defile the marriage bed and taint the gift that was intended for our husband.

In a society that promotes casual, uncommitted sex, we have to make a choice to abstain remembering that sex wasn't created to be casual. Each time you lie with someone who is not your husband, you create a new soul tie and give away another piece of yourself that should be reserved for God and your husband. A soul tie is a link between two people in the spiritual realm that can have positive or negative effects. When you consecrate your marriage and create a soul tie with your husband, you please God and allow him to use you two as one in the spirit. A negative impact of a soul tie is being spiritually connected with someone who is detrimental to your emotional, physical, or mental health. An example is a woman who has had sex outside of marriage and the man has moved on to the next one or cheated on her, abused her, or stolen from her.

The reason many unmarried women stay in situations

they don't belong in is soul ties, spiritual connections that can be so strong that even when they get married, they're held back by their past soul ties. Though they have no desire to see or be with their past lovers they can't let go of the hurt and pain they were caused because they affected them so deeply and their souls are intertwined.

Negative soul ties can be overcome through deliverance and healing by God, but this is why purity is so important; it prevents negative soul ties from happening in the first place. When you keep yourself pure, you prevent yourself from developing bad soul ties, this is important because the deeply spiritual but negative connections you make can end up driving your decisions. The things you allow into your spirit build your character, and they could be things that make it difficult for you to connect with God. Each time you put yourself out there and get hurt, the wall you build for defense gets higher. But God says that if you trust him and walk in his way, he will lay the foundation of your heart and protect it. When you spiritually commit to being Jesus's bride, he will help you on your journey of purity because he loves you and wants you to have a strong, stable foundation. If you won't allow Jesus to call you "wifey," why would you allow a man to do that?

Today, wifey has become a common term to define a woman who is wife material but remains in girlfriend status. We don't want to have a temporary commitment to Jesus; that's not his desire. He died so we would be his wife, not his wifey, and have a permanent covenant with him. So why do we settle for temporary commitments from men and allow them to give us titles that ultimately lead nowhere? God had plans for us from the beginning, and when Jesus came to earth, he knew the plan was to lay down his life to enter a covenant with us. He took time to prepare for his ultimate sacrifice; he knew the purpose and proclaimed it boldly and in truth. We should expect the same from a man; he should have a plan and proclaim it boldly and in truth.

As I mentioned earlier our purity is not just sexual; there are some who have remained sexually pure but not emotionally or spiritually pure. Purity involves keeping our hearts and minds as pure as our bodies. We should not allow ourselves to be corrupted by the lies someone tells us to get what he wants. We should recognize when the spirit of someone we are with is toxic; the spirit we have as the bride of Christ will allow us to do that. Being unequally yoked has a real effect on our purity; if we're not careful, temptation and sin can overtake us.

The only way we remain pure in heart and in spirit is by trusting God to sustain us. Our prayer should be this: "God, we thank you for making us emotional and sexual beings, but Father, help us abstain from whatever is outside your will. Lord, cover me in your blood and keep me under your wing. Help me remember that I am not alone and that all things work together for the good of those who love you. If there's anything in me that is not of you, or any area I need to fix before marriage, Lord, have your way. Help me, Lord, to keep your Commandments and remain pure in mind, body, and spirit until you send me my husband."

One thing to note about the last line of that prayer—"my husband." Know that God will *not* give you someone else's husband. If you're sleeping with someone else's husband or waiting for him to marry you, realize you're not in God's will and you need to stop it now! While it may be possible that the person God designed for you married the wrong person, trust that God won't deliver him to you while he's married. We serve a God of order, and there's nothing orderly about delivering you a married man.

When you lie with a married man, you're defiling his marriage bed and the one you may hope to have with him. You're in an adulterous situation, and you're worth more than that. Deuteronomy 7:6 reads, "For you are a people holy to the LORD your God. The LORD your God has chosen you out of all the peoples on the face of the earth to be his people, his treasured possession." And Proverbs 31:10 says, "A wife of noble character who can find? She is worth far more than rubies." You are God's treasured possession worth far more than rubies. Do not allow any impurity to taint your character.

FOOD FOR THOUGHT

1. Who or what have I allowed to affect my purity? Do I care more about that than God?
2. Am I ready to subdue my flesh and turn my will over to God so I can live blamelessly in my singleness? Why or why not? If I am not, what do I need to change so I can be ready?
3. Do I think it's okay to play house with no commitment knowing that the most powerful man to ever walk the earth couldn't wait to make me his bride and shed his blood to confirm that covenant? Is the man I lie next to every night who is uncertain of the destination of our lives worth my purity?

8

LOVE

Love—strong affection for another arising out of kinship or personal ties; attraction based on sexual desire; affection and tenderness felt by lovers; the object of attachment, devotion, or admiration; unselfish loyal and benevolent concern for the good of another as the fatherly concern of God for humankind and brotherly concern for others; a person's adoration of God.

Early on when we were courting, my husband and I had a discussion in which he claimed women were better at commitments and men were better at love. He said that a woman would stay committed to a man even if she no longer loved him and that a man could love a woman even though he wasn't committed to her.

I could see where he was coming from. Our discussion prompted us to study the difference between love and commitment. What we found is that love and commitment are one and the same. When you love someone, if you truly take on the biblical definition of love, you make a commitment to that person and love him in all he does and in all he is.

We woman often operate on conditional love. It may start out unconditional and last for years, but then something happens. We feel our needs aren't being met, and love erodes; it becomes conditional on the happiness we feel. When love starts to fade, anger, animosity, and disrespect take its place. One minute, we're in love, and the next minute, just his voice bothers us and the things we once did to show our love and support go by the wayside. That was me!

Prior to marrying my husband, I had a few relationships in which I loved hard. I was committed to whomever I was dating at the time, and there wasn't anything I wouldn't do for that man. But over time during these relationships, something would change. Someone who seemed to excite me and make me feel special suddenly made me feel scared, worthless, controlled, or just plain old bored. I found myself in relationship after relationship struggling to determine who I was and what I wanted out of the relationship.

People said things to me that broke me mentally and spiritually. After a while, I started thinking something was wrong with me. I became convinced no one would ever want to be with me because of my imperfections, because I had too much mouth, because my attitude was bad. It didn't seem to matter where I met a man—church, a store, a club—the result was the same. I began to think I deserved to be mistreated because my frustration with them grew over time, and then I responded with a bad attitude. In many of my relationships, I didn't always act in love as a result of how the one I loved made me feel despite my commitment and loyalty. Part of me felt he didn't deserve my love. This mental and emotional abuse angered me and caused me to struggle with who I thought I was and whom they said I was. That changed my mind-set and pulled me further from God.

Then one day, I had an encounter with God. He revealed to me just how toxic my way of handling relationships was. I wasn't showing love to those I dated, and I didn't love myself. I had to decide to stay in that mind-set and allow the brokenness and abuse to continue or step out on faith and trust the love of God to carry me through. I chose to break free from all the abuse and negative experiences I'd been having and thinking I deserved to be mistreated. God showed me that I was important and worthy of love because of the love he had for me. He reminded me that I was special and that I was not defined by what man says but by what he said.

Since making that decision, I have been able to love unconditionally. When I took the step to love myself and trust God, I found forgiveness in my heart for those who had hurt me and had me bound in that hurt.

In 1 John 4:20, we read, "Whoever claims to love God yet hates a brother or sister is a liar. For whoever does not love their brother and sister, whom they have seen, cannot love God, whom they have not seen." Though I had experienced pain in previous relationships, I knew I couldn't walk in malice or anger; I knew I had to forgive, and true forgiveness comes by understanding what God says about love. When we give pieces of ourselves away prior to marriage, we can end up facing many challenges. Thankfully, I came to know, understand, and apply the love of God to my life; that's freed me from the pain of my past and has made it easier to show love to my husband properly.

The lesson of love is the hardest lesson I had to learn, but it was one of the most critical lessons I learned. Knowing what I know now, I believe failure to learn this lesson diminishes your chances for a successful marriage. Marriage is forever; you have to love through the good and bad, and if you don't know the true meaning of love, you may struggle and fail.

As I got to know my husband, I realized it was important for me to love him in God's way. He is so deserving of it not because of himself but because I know whose he is. Since I profess to love God, I must also love him. Prior to meeting him, I was already coming into the understanding that I was the bride of Christ and was becoming comfortable in Christ's love for me. My understanding and application of love flourished as we courted and got engaged. My husband and I faced many challenges and attacks that could have conquered us had it not been for our love. My husband, a strong Christian, helped me stay rooted in love and often challenged me with the Word when I wasn't walking in love.

If you don't remain pure, that opens the door for issues when you finally meet the right one. The devil uses everything you have said or done against you, and if you and your partner don't know God, trust God, and have his love in your hearts, that can overtake your relationship.

What is the love of God? First, we need to understand that God *is* love; love is an essential part of his character. His love endures forever, sacrifices, and goes beyond anything we can understand. We have to understand how much God loves us before we can truly love someone. Though it's hard to understand why, God loved us so much that he sent Jesus to live a blameless life and die for our sakes. We see God's enduring love in the fact that Jesus rose from the dead. All of this is unbelievable because we know we're sinners who have done nothing to deserve the love he has for us. That's the love he calls us to walk in. Whether people around us deserve our love or not, we should love them and be an example of God's love for us.

In 1 Corinthians 13:1–8, God gave us the characteristics of his love. Though I have studied this in depth, I'm still learning to walk fully in his love, but I am committed to trying. In my commitment, I feel God changing me and my attitude. Verses 1 and 2 of 1 Corinthians 15 says that faith without love is nothing. If we profess to have faith and be committed to God and have the gifts of the spirit but not love, we have nothing! This is confirmed by the scripture I noted earlier in which God said that if we claim to love him but don't love our brothers and sisters, we're liars.

Verse 3 describes being committed but having no love. If we serve the community, help friends, or are kind to someone but have no love, we gain nothing. So many times, we pretend to like someone or do things for accolades, but God is saying that if we do these things but do not truly love or do it with love, we gain nothing. People can tell the real from the fake; when we show people genuine love, that creates an opportunity for us to evangelize and share the love of God with them. That's the ultimate gain!

The passage tells us what love is—patient, kind, doesn't envy, doesn't boast, not proud, doesn't dishonor others, not self-seeking, not easily angered, no record of wrongs, doesn't delight in evil, rejoices in truth, protects, trusts, hopes, perseveres, and never fails. This is the love God has for us and calls us to have for others. In our marriage with Christ, we learn grace and mercy. We learn to love God in this way, and that love translates into how we love others.

When you decide you want to get married and be in love as a woman of God, you're saying you want to love others as God loves you. The worldview of love declares that as long as you make me happy, I'll love you, but God says, "No matter the circumstances, no matter what you do or say, even when you don't deserve love, I love you, and I call on you to love others the same way." Love is selfless and requires daily commitment.

FOOD FOR THOUGHT

1. Do you love yourself? Do you love God? Do you understand the love God has for you? If you don't love yourself, spend time with God and learn to love yourself because you cannot love anyone else if you don't love yourself.
2. Are you truly ready to love selflessly and accept others with all their faults? Are you ready to make a daily commitment to love? Are you ready for "Till death do us part"?
3. Have you been hurt so badly that you don't know where to begin with loving someone else and sharing your heart?

9

RESPECT

Respect—high or special regard; the quality or state of being esteemed; an act of giving particular attention.

Wives, in the same way submit yourselves to your own husbands so that, if any of them do not believe the word, they may be won over without words by the behavior of their wives, when they see the purity and reverence of your lives. Your beauty should not come from outward adornment, such as elaborate hairstyles and the wearing of gold jewelry or fine clothes. Rather, it should be that of your inner self, the unfading beauty of a gentle and quiet spirit, which is of great worth in God's sight. For this is the way the holy women of the past who put their hope in God used to adorn themselves. They submitted themselves to their own husbands, like Sarah, who obeyed Abraham and called him her lord. You are her daughters if you

do what is right and do not give way to fear.
(1 Peter 3:1–6)

The Bible calls on us as wives to respect and submit to our husbands. In today's society, we lack the ability to submit because of many reasons, but one main reason is that there's a lack of respect between the sexes. Men lack respect for women, and women lack respect for men.

We've bought into the worldly standards of what a good man looks like—wealthy, good looking, a career-oriented and self-sufficient provider. Any man who doesn't fit this bill is often treated with less respect than one who does. A man can be abusive and mistreat women, but because of his status, we may choose to respect him more than a man who is a work in progress.

In our independence, we women have excelled and reached new heights in the workplace to the point that we are often more self-sufficient than our counterparts are. Some of us no longer respect men who makes less than we do, or who live with their mothers, or who work at jobs we consider beneath us.

Many of us don't realize how disrespectful we are. I know I didn't. Did you know that simply changing the way we say things, we can make something sound respectful or disrespectful? As I neared my wedding day, I focused heavily on the characteristics God laid out for a wife. In the passage above, God tells us to submit. Submission in a relationship is a form of respect; it gives a man the opportunity to be a man. This doesn't mean you can't have thoughts, feelings, or emotions, but it does mean understanding that the man is the leader of the family and respecting him in that role. That means that if he makes a decision you don't agree with, you don't go against his word, you support it. It also means that if it fails, you don't throw that in his face. It means that if you have been more successful in your career or finances, you should be willing to support him; you should afford him whatever resources God has afforded you because you are his helpmeet. When you marry, two become one. As we say, what's his is ours and what's ours is his.

Before you get married, you should pray about how God would have you support your husband understanding that when you are married, submission is a command. Submission is not about devaluing yourself; it's about understanding your role in the marriage. A wife who understands her role in marriage is tremendously valuable. The ability to be humble is valuable. Allowing your husband room to grow and change is valuable. This is what we wives are called to; our roles as wives are valuable and just as critical to the success of the family as that of our husbands.

God also says they should see purity and reverence in your lives; this is value. This display of respect is not toward man but toward God. When you treat God with respect and follow his commands, your husband cannot deny his power. Men are not stupid; they know when they are wrong, and they know when they are being a pain, but when you show them love and respect and submit to their authority not because of them but because of your relationship with God, he will take notice. This goes back to the beginning of the book and trusting God versus trusting man. Even after marriage, you are called to have a relationship with God; you are first dependent on God but also dependent on your husband. Your husband is your earthly covering and is to be respected in the same way you respect God. Your marriage to man should resemble the marriage you have with Christ before you were married.

We are also called to have a gentle and quiet spirit. Let's be honest—in our proclaimed independence, we are not often gentle or quiet. Since we had to fight so hard to get where we are as women, we're more often bold and outspoken. We've decided not to take anyone's stuff; we will be heard, we will have power, and we will not budge. Many times, this results in us using our words to tear down our man. We feel an urge to call out every issue and to beat the point to death. This is me, and it is something I'm working on daily. I have seen the effect my words have had on previous relationships and my current relationship. It could only be due to God's love flowing through my husband that he married me despite my mouth.

I have gotten so much better, but when we first started dating, I often said things that hurt him. And it wasn't always what I said but the manner in which I said it. We don't realize how disrespectful we can be with our words. Submission, purity, and reverence deal more with our actions, but a gentle and quiet spirit deals with our words. I can hear you saying, "I'm not being quiet for anyone. I'm gonna speak my mind." Go ahead. You'll speak yourself right out of a husband.

Proverbs 18:21 says, "The tongue has the power of life and death, and those who love it will eat its fruit." James 3:6, 9–10 says,

> The tongue also is a fire, a world of evil among the parts of the body. It corrupts the whole body, sets the whole course of one's life on fire, and is itself set on fire by hell. With the tongue we praise our Lord and Father, and with it we curse human beings, who have been made in God's likeness. Out of the same mouth come praise and cursing. My brothers and sisters, this should not be.

My brothers and sisters, in the same way that we cannot profess to love God and hate our brother, we cannot use our tongue to praise God while we curse our brother. We have to understand that even when we don't feel like it, we have to be mindful of our words. In the same way our loving words can draw a man in, our hurtful words can push him away.

Out of respect for the one you love, it's better not to say everything that comes to your mind. If it needs to be said, be thoughtful about how you say it. I've had difficult conversations with my husband about things concerning me or decisions he made. When I wasn't careful with my words, our conversation erupted into an argument, but when I operated with a gentle spirit and thoughtful words, he understood my point, and even if he didn't agree, my voice was at least heard and he could not call me disrespectful.

Our husbands desire to be respected in words and action just as we do. We should not allow our independence to cause us to be disrespectful. We wouldn't dare treat Christ with disrespect, so we shouldn't treat our earthly husbands that way. If you're saying to yourself, *I'll be all these things after I get married*, you missed the point—you do not become a wife when you marry a man; you are already Christ's wife. That relationship should transform your character and prompt you to walk in purity, love, and respect.

FOOD FOR THOUGHT

1. Do you respect God? Do you respect yourself? If you don't, ask yourself why or why not.
2. Think over your current and previous relationships; have you ever been disrespectful? Are you a disrespectful person in general?
3. What do you need to submit to God to change your attitude? Is it your pride, independence, selfishness, attitude?
4. What do you gain by being disrespectful, loud, or rude?

COVERING

Covering—something that covers or conceals; to guard from attack; to deal with.

I say this with boldness—if you aren't prepared to be a covering then you are not prepared to be married. In the same way that Christ died to cover all our sins, we wives are to cover our husbands. This doesn't mean that we lay down our lives for them as Christ did for us but that we cover them with prayer and petitions to the Father.

In 1 Timothy 12:1, we are encouraged to make prayers of supplication, intercession, and thanksgiving for all people. Being married to Christ, we have an opportunity to learn to pray for ourselves. We are human, so we fall short, and so will our future husbands. It is not our job to fix them but to pray to the Lord and allow the transformational power of the Holy Spirit to change them.

Too often, we women try to mold men into what we desire them to be; we should let God shape them into the men he has designed for us. His molding and shaping may take longer than we'd like, but we should trust God. Even before you meet your husband, you should be interceding and praying on his behalf. You should pray that his heart will be whole and have the love of God flowing through it, that he would be protected from harm and wise in his decision making. You should pray every prayer you would make for yourself in your marriage to Christ for your husband to be as well.

Love protects and keeps no record of wrongs; we should exhibit those qualities. This speaks of how we talk about them to our friends, family, and others. Do you lift him up or put him down? If others observe you treating him with respect, then even if he doesn't deserve respect, they will honor him in an effort to honor you.

This concept of being a covering is one I discovered in my time leading up to marriage. During one of our counseling sessions, I threw my fiancé under the bus. I mean, it was speeding down the road and I pushed him right in front of it. This really hurt him, which in turn hurt me. I didn't even mean to do it or realize that I had done it until he explained it to me. This isn't to say we cannot seek godly counsel and have real conversations about real issues in a relationship, but as I said when talking about respect—presentation is everything. The issue was something we had talked about and dealt with, but I brought it up in a manner that showed I was keeping a record of wrongs. When this topic came up, I offloaded every frustration about it even though I had claimed to have forgiven him. As his covering, I did the wrong thing. I should have protected him, and I should not have kept the record of wrongs after saying I had forgiven him. I realized that the issue was really my own because though he had done something to hurt me, I was the one holding onto the pain and dwelling on the situation. There was a shift in my attitude; love was fighting to come through.

We both learned that we had to be constantly praying for one another. As challenges and disagreements arise, the devil wants you to harp on those things. He will constantly bring them to your mind to create discord in your relationship, but by covering each other in prayer and love, you can combat Satan's lies with truth. When you know the truth, the way you talk about an issue is different. The truth about what God has spoken about an area of your relationship will cause you to speak with positivity though the issue may be a touchy subject. It will cause you to speak with peace and hope. Understand that the devil's goal is to destroy your marriage before it starts; it's no different than him trying to destroy your relationship with Christ. He wants you to believe his lies instead of God's truth. He doesn't want you to be positive or hopeful but rather lonely and negative. For this reason, you have to be on the watch for the tricks of the enemy even as disagreements arise in your relationship. You have to be able to assess whether this is a real issue and what you are even arguing about. Too often, couples do not cover each other; they leave themselves susceptible to the enemy's tricks.

As we talk about being a covering, understand that this is possible only when you are in a relationship with Christ. If you are not allowing yourself to be covered by the blood of Jesus, you leave yourself vulnerable to the enemy. The devil used Judas to betray Jesus; if we are not careful, he can use us to carry out his tasks even though we know God. Again, he who finds a wife finds a good thing. If a wife is to be a covering, she must know how to pray and combat the enemy's lies with truth.

All this training comes from your relationship with Christ. You are a beautiful woman who is married before marriage. Use your singleness to get to know God, to study his Word, to understand who he has declared you to be. Learn to pray and intercede for others. Desire to serve God in spirit and in truth in your singleness and in your marriage.

In your independence, do not forget that you are dependent on God. Remember that you are the bride of Christ. Remember to trust God and his process. He will never leave you or forsake you.

Food for Thought

1. What does my prayer life look like? Do I pray for myself? Am I ready to pray for someone else?
2. Do I trust God with my heart and prayers? Do I believe God will supply all my needs?
3. Am I ready to relinquish the control of changing man to God? Do I understand that it has never been my place to mold man?

References

1. Pain. 2011. In Merriam-Webster.com. Retrieved January 12, 2017, from https://www.merriam-webster.com/dictionary/pain.
2. Independent. 2011. In Merriam-Webster.com. Retrieved January 12, 2017, from https://www.merriam-webster.com/dictionary/independent.
3. Dependent. 2011. In Merriam-Webster.com. Retrieved January 12, 2017, from https://www.merriam-webster.com/dictionary/dependent.
4. Bride. 2011. In Merriam-Webster.com. Retrieved January 12, 2017, from https://www.merriam-webster.com/dictionary/bride.
5. Trust. 2011. In Merriam-Webster.com. Retrieved January 12, 2017, from https://www.merriam-webster.com/dictionary/trust.
6. Courting. 2011. In Merriam-Webster.com. Retrieved January 12, 2017, from https://www.merriam-webster.com/dictionary/courting.
7. Purity. 2011. In Merriam-Webster.com. Retrieved January 12, 2017, from https://www.merriam-webster.com/dictionary/purity.

8. Love. 2011. In Merriam-Webster.com. Retrieved January 12, 2017, from https://www.merriam-webster.com/dictionary/love.

9. Respect. 2011. In Merriam-Webster.com. Retrieved January 12, 2017, from https://www.merriam-webster.com/dictionary/respect.

10. Covering. 2011. In Merriam-Webster.com. Retrieved January 12, 2017, from https://www.merriam-webster.com/dictionary/covering.

11. Harris, J. (2012). *I Kissed Dating Goodbye A New Attitude Toward Relationships and Romance*. New York, WaterBrook Multnomah an imprint of the Crown Publishing Group a company of Random House Inc.